THE TERRIBLE SUPER SAD DAY

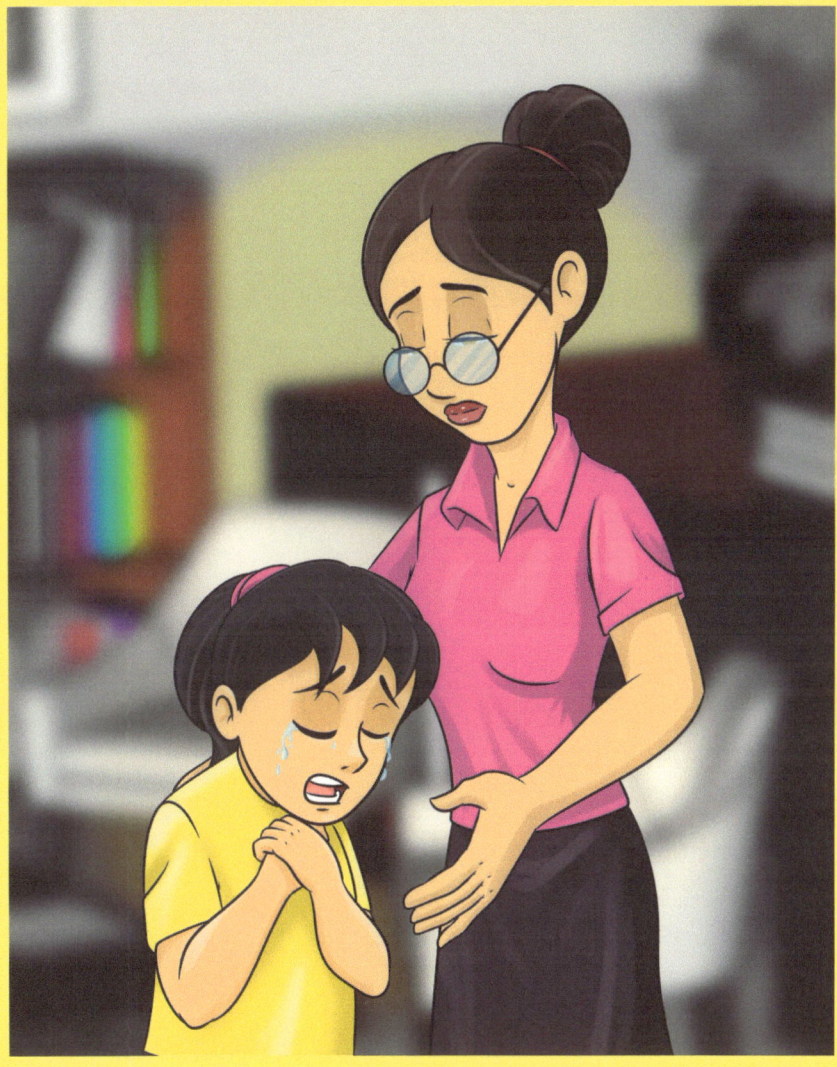

VANESSA VALLES LCSW-S
ILLUSTRATED BY VICTOR GUIZA

The Terrible, Super Sad Day
All Rights Reserved.
Copyright © 2025 Vanessa Valles LCSW-S
v2.0

This is a work of fiction. The events and characters described herein are imaginary and are not intended to refer to specific places or living persons. The opinions expressed in this manuscript are solely the opinions of the author and do not represent the opinions or thoughts of the publisher. The author has represented and warranted full ownership and/or legal right to publish all the materials in this book.

This book may not be reproduced, transmitted, or stored in whole or in part by any means, including graphic, electronic, or mechanical without the express written consent of the publisher except in the case of brief quotations embodied in critical articles and reviews.

Outskirts Press, Inc.
http://www.outskirtspress.com

ISBN: 978-1-9772-7513-4

Illustrations by: Victor Guiza
Illustrations © 2025 Vanessa Valles LCSW-S. All rights reserved - used with permission.

Outskirts Press and the "OP" logo are trademarks belonging to Outskirts Press, Inc.

PRINTED IN THE UNITED STATES OF AMERICA

This Book Belongs to:

_____

Isabella was a happy girl. She lived in a house with her mom, dad, brothers, and sisters. It was a sunny day outside. She had gone to the store with her parents.

Her mothaer's phone rang and her mom began to cry. They were big tears the size of one hundred raindrops. *Oh no*, Isabella thought.

Her mom told the family they had to leave the store and go to the hospital. Isabella climbed into the family car. Isabella was scared. She had never seen her mom cry.

When they arrived at the hospital, they went inside and sat in the waiting room. Isabella saw her dad hug her mom. Isabella was scared and wanted a hug too. She walked towards her mother and father, and they gave her a big hug.

"What's wrong?" Isabella asked. Her father responded and said, "There was an accident, someone we love was hurt. The doctor asked us to come to the hospital." Isabella was worried. She felt it in her stomach, and it felt full and queasy. She felt it in her chest. Her heart was beating very fast. She felt it in her hands. They were very hot and sweaty.

Isabella's mom was called to the other room by doctors. Isabella's mom asked her brothers, sisters, and Isabella to sit in the lobby with their dad and watch TV. Isabella was curious what the doctor had to say. She was glad they had called her mom to the other room. She liked it better when her mom got really big, important news first. Her mother always knew how to explain it to her.

Isabella tried to watch the TV but she just could not concentrate. All she could do was stare at the door. She tried to keep her mind busy. Isabella counted how many circles were on each piece of tile on the floor. Isabella counted every line on the clock. Isabella counted every leaf on the plant. *What's taking so long?* Isabella wondered.

Finally, the door opened. It was Isabella's mother. She was still crying. Her teardrops were not as big. Isabella's mom talked to the family. She told them what had happened. Everyone was sad. Isabella thought, *What a terrible, super sad day.* Isabella didn't cry. She wondered what that meant.

That night Isabella went home and lay in bed. She tried to go to sleep but sleep never came. She counted sheep. She counted stars. Nothing worked. She just kept thinking about what her mom had told her and she felt sad. The feeling in her stomach and chest were still there. Finally, without even knowing it, Isabella went to sleep.

The next day Isabella woke up and felt normal for one short minute ... until she remembered what happened yesterday. Then Isabella felt sad. Isabella's mom told her she would not go to school this week. She explained that Isabella needed time to process and understand everything that had happened. She shared that they would spend time together with family and friends.

Isabella spent that week visiting family and friends. She got a lot of hugs from her mom and her dad. Some days Isabella cried a tear or two. Isabella wondered where her tears were. Isabella felt sad but her tears never came.

After the week passed, Isabella went back to school. Her friends wanted to play, and Isabella wanted to play too, but she just felt tired. She sat down and stared at the trees and looked at the clouds.

Isabella went home and didn't want to watch TV. She just wanted to sleep. Isabella felt sad. Isabella was normally easy to get along with, but some days when things got bad Isabella would start to scream and throw or snatch things.

Isabella's mother and father made an appointment. They took her to go see a counselor. Her counselor's name was Ms. Vanessa. Isabella was not sure what to expect; she had never seen a counselor before. The counselor, Ms. Vanessa, explained that she was there to help and to listen. She explained that sometimes sad things happen and that it's hard to understand. Talking about how we feel helps us find ways to better cope with our feelings.

The counselor, Ms. Vanessa, was nice. She wore glasses; she had a big pile of books on her desk and a big comfortable brown couch. Isabella liked the counselor, Ms. Vanessa. She went to see Ms. Vanessa every week for five months.

The counselor, Ms. Vanessa, talked to Isabella and taught her different things. Sometimes they would play a game and laugh. Ms. Vanessa would ask Isabella questions about important people in Isabella's life and ask her to share stories of her experiences with them. Sometimes when Isabella shared memories she would feel sad or angry, but most times she felt happy.

The counselor, Ms. Vanessa, taught Isabella how to develop coping skills. Ms. Vanessa said coping skills were like tools for her toolbox on how to deal with life. Ms. Vanessa taught Isabella how to do deep breathing so Isabella could hold her breath and feel the air in her stomach. The counselor, Ms. Vanessa, taught her to breathe like she was blowing up a big imaginary balloon full of air; she said that would help when Isabella's chest and heart felt anxiety. Together, they counted 4 seconds in and 4 seconds out. Isabella's balloon was so big she thought it was going to pop!

The counselor, Ms. Vanessa, taught Isabella how to ground herself by using her five senses; this was helpful if she had a hard time managing her anxiety, focusing in class, or if she felt upset. Isabella got to practice with the counselor, Ms. Vanessa, and that was fun. Isabella talked about what she saw, felt, tasted, smelled, and heard.

Isabella had a bad day and threw everything in her room on the floor and yelled at the top of her lungs. Isabella didn't know why she was mad. Ms. Vanessa taught Isabella about different ways to express herself when she was upset other than yelling or throwing things. Ms. Vanessa gave Isabella a journal where she could draw or write her feelings. She also taught Isabella that it was okay to take a time-out and relax by a window and then try to solve her problem later. They created a feelings chart and mood diary, and talked about a problem-solving model Isabella could use.

The counselor, Ms. Vanessa, let Isabella talk about the "terrible, super sad day." When Isabella told Ms. Vanessa, she cried a lot. There were so many tears that Isabella thought she could fill a river. There were some thoughts that Isabella's counselor explained might need to change. They talked about ways to think healthy thoughts that helped Isabella heal. That evening, Ms. Vanessa asked Isabella's mom and dad to give her hugs and kisses. Isabella's mom slept in Isabella's room with her that night. Both her mom and dad told Isabella they loved her. They gave her big hugs. Isabella felt loved. She felt safe.

The counselor, Ms. Vanessa, taught Isabella to use art to express her feelings. Isabella created a lovely drawing of a bird. She told Ms. Vanessa it was to remind her that even when birds are tired and they stop flying, they always spread their wings and fly again, soaring high in the sky. Isabella said the bird reminded her that she could take a break when she was tired, and once she felt better, she could spread her wings and fly again too. Ms. Vanessa knew Isabella was learning to take one day at a time.

Isabella liked talking with the counselor, Ms. Vanessa. After several months of going to see Ms. Vanessa, she asked Isabella's mom and dad to join them on the next visit. Ms. Vanessa told Isabella the visit was to talk about how well she was doing. The next week Isabella went in to see Ms. Vanessa, and her mom and dad were there too. Ms. Vanessa asked them how they felt the visits were going and asked how Isabella was doing at home and at school. Everyone said Isabella was doing better; everyone was happy. Isabella was feeling more like herself again.

The counselor, Ms. Vanessa, told them that based on their reports and feedback she was getting in the counseling sessions, Isabella was doing well on her road to feeling and living healthy. Ms. Vanessa said she felt like it was an okay time to end therapy.

Isabella was sad she wasn't going to see Ms. Vanessa anymore. Ms. Vanessa told her, "Isabella, you are a very special girl. I am very proud of you. You have done such a good job learning how to use the techniques we talked about to feel better. Now I get to help another little girl or boy who doesn't feel well. If you ever need to talk to me again, you can always come back to see me." Isabella was happy to hear she could see Ms. Vanessa again one day if she needed to.

That day, Isabella and her mom and dad stopped for ice cream on the way home. Isabella sat down to eat her ice cream and felt happy. Her mom smiled, her dad smiled, and Isabella laughed.

Isabella's mom and dad were happy Isabella felt better. Isabella was happy she had people who loved her. The memory from the very terrible, super sad day they'd had several months ago was still there, but Isabella felt like she could breathe again. Isabella knew she was loved, and she felt safe.

Everyone was happy.

The End!

Best ways to use this book: This book was written to help caregivers and clinicians relate to children who are experiencing dysregulation in their mental wellness and mental stability following a critical event. This book can be used for planned or unplanned loss, deaths, medical events, disasters, and traumas. This is also an effective therapeutic tool that can be used as a social story to help children understand their experience, understand what they are feeling, recognize their symptoms, and utilize basic coping strategies that may be helpful in managing their emotional responses. It can also be effective in helping them understand what to expect in therapy.

Common Symptoms Following a Traumatic Event

- Physical Symptoms: Chills, fatigue, nausea, vomiting, chest pain, headaches, elevated blood pressure, rapid heart rate, muscle tremors, shock symptoms, difficulty breathing
- Cognitive Symptoms: Disorientation, slowed thinking, poor concentration, confusion, decreased attention span, uncertainty, nightmares, difficulty concentrating, poor ability to retain information or complete tasks, missing deadlines
- Emotional Symptoms: Anxiety, fear, grief, depression, withdrawal, irritability, resentfulness, tearfulness, feeling of being overwhelmed, frustration, guilt, sense of loss, anger, denial
- Behavioral Symptoms: Emotional outbursts, change in activity level, disturbed sleep, increase in smoking, being easily startled, hypervigilance, antisocial behavior, being fidgety, difficulty relaxing

Tips for Coping with a Traumatic Event

- Ask for support from people who care about you.
- Communicate your experience in whatever ways feel comfortable to you.
- Join a local support group or therapy group.
- Eat a well-balanced meal and get plenty of rest.
- Work the stress out of the body by walking, dancing, doing yard work, etc.
- Practice relaxation techniques such as deep breathing, stretching, yoga, mindfulness, meditation, visualization, progressive muscle relaxation.

- Establishing or reestablishing healthy routines can be helpful.
- Avoid drugs, alcohol, or any mood- or mind-altering substance.
- Avoid major life decisions if possible.
- Develop effective coping skills (for stress management, self-care, social support, peer support).
- Develop a self-care plan that includes strategies for building resilience (e.g., get regular exercise, set aside quiet time for meditation or relaxation).
- Practice your spiritual beliefs and engage with a faith leader or group for support.
- Seek care from a licensed, trained, trauma-informed provider who can recognize your symptoms and offer evidence-based treatment and guidance.

<u>Helpful Coping Skills</u>

- Positive Reframing: It's natural to feel there are no positives in your loss. Try focusing on the memories that keep you connected to the people you love during the loss.
- Journaling: Try journaling about how you feel.
- Gardening: Consider making a memorial garden or planting forget-me-not flowers.
- Mindfulness: Practice mindfulness and allow yourself to be present, and clear your thoughts if you are experiencing ruminations that feel unhelpful.
- Art Therapy: Consider a collage, painting, or drawing of something that connects you to your loved one.
- Music Therapy: Listen to music that helps you process emotions or lifts your mood or spirit.
- Prepare for anniversaries—the anniversary of the event, someone passing, important dates (birthdays, holidays, anniversaries, graduations, etc.). Take time off, spend time with loved ones, plan group activities such as story and memory sharing, balloon release, dove releases, scattering of flowers or ashes.
- Create new traditions: Be intentional about moving forward. You can't stay connected to rituals and memories from the past forever while moving forward. Be intentional about embracing new experiences and new traditions with the people in your life who care about you.

Milton Keynes UK
Ingram Content Group UK Ltd.
UKHW051514131124
451151UK00002B/17